Native Americans

The Blackfoot

Barbara A. Gray-Kanatiiosh

ABDO Publishing Company

visit us at
www.abdopub.com

Published by ABDO Publishing Company, 4940 Viking Drive, Suite 622, Edina, Minnesota 55435. Copyright © 2002 Abdo Consulting Group, Inc. International copyrights reserved in all countries. No part of this book may be reproduced in any form without written permission from the publisher.

Printed in the United States.

Illustrations: David Kanietakeron Fadden
Interior Photos: Corbis
Editors: Bob Italia, Tamara L. Britton, Kate A. Furlong, Kristin Van Cleaf
Art Direction & Maps: Neil Klinepier

Library of Congress Cataloging-in-Publication Data

Gray-Kanatiiosh, Barbara A., 1963-
   The Blackfoot / Barbara A. Gray-Kanatiiosh
     p. cm. -- (Native Americans)
   Includes index.
   Summary: An introduction to the history and past and present social life and customs of the Blackfoot Indians, an Algonquian tribe of North America.
   ISBN 1-57765-604-0
   1. Siksika Indians--History--Juvenile literature. 2. Siksika Indians--Social life and customs--Juvenile literature.[1. Siksika Indians. 2. Indians of North America.] I. Title. II. Native Americans (Edina, Minn.)

E99.S54 G73 2002
978'. 004973--dc21

2001045895

About the Author: Barbara A. Gray-Kanatiiosh, JD

Barbara Gray-Kanatiiosh, JD, is an Akwesasne Mohawk. She has a Juris Doctorate from Arizona State University, where she was one of the first recipients of ASU's special certificate in Indian Law. She is currently pursuing a PhD in Justice Studies at ASU and is focusing on Native American issues. Barbara works hard to educate children about Native Americans through her writing and Web site where children may ask questions and receive a written response about the Haudenosaunee culture. The Web site is: www.peace4turtleisland.org

Illustrator: David Kanietakeron Fadden

David Kanietakeron Fadden is a member of the Akwesasne Mohawk Wolf Clan. His work has appeared in publications such as *Akwesasne Notes*, *Indian Time*, and the *Northeast Indian Quarterly*. Examples of his work have also appeared in various publications of the Six Nations Indian Museum in Onchiota, NY. His work has also appeared in "How The West Was Lost: Always The Enemy," produced by Gannett Production which appeared on the Discovery Channel. David's work has been exhibited in Albany, NY; the Lake Placid Center for the Arts; Centre Strathearn in Montreal, Quebec; North Country Community College in Saranac Lake, NY; Paul Smith's College in Paul Smiths, NY; and at the Unison Arts & Learning Center in New Paltz, NY.

Contents

Where They Lived 4
Society 6
Food 8
Homes 10
Clothing 12
Crafts 14
Family 16
Children 18
Myths 20
War 22
Contact with Europeans 24
Crowfoot 26
The Blackfoot Today 28
Glossary 31
Web Sites 31
Index 32

Where They Lived

The Blackfoot called themselves Niitsitapii (neet-sit-ah-pee), which means the Real People. They were a **confederacy** of three tribes. The tribes were called the Siksika (sik-seek-ah), the Kainai (kai-nah), and the Pikuni (pik-oo-nee). The Blackfoot spoke Pikuni, a language in the Algonquian family.

The Blackfoot lived in present-day northern Montana and southern Canada. Their land covered a large area. Blackfoot territory may have reached from present-day North Dakota west to the Rocky Mountains. To the north, their land

Glaciated mountain peaks in Northern Montana

reached Alberta and Saskatchewan in Canada. The Blackfoot homelands had high, rolling plains. It also had forests, grasslands, streams, and rivers. Hills, rugged glaciers, and steep cliffs also covered the land.

The Blackfoot Homelands

Society

The Blackfoot lived together in **bands**. Each band had from 80 to 240 people. The members worked together to feed and defend the people. If people were unhappy with their group, they were free to leave and join another band.

Each band's people chose a chief. He had to be a good warrior, and generous to his people. Each band also had a war chief, a peace chief, and a council of elders.

Blackfoot bands had many societies. The members of each society had special duties. The military societies protected the people and enforced the traditional laws. The religious societies and women's societies performed ceremonies.

Holy men and women were spiritual advisers. They also healed the people. Holy people received gifts in exchange for their medicinal help.

Occasionally Blackfoot bands gathered together. They joined forces to protect their land and people from harm. The chiefs often met to discuss important matters. The Blackfoot also gathered for special ceremonies, such as the Sun Dance.

A Blackfoot band's tipis

Food

    The Blackfoot hunted and gathered their food. They hunted moose, elk, deer, rabbit, pronghorn, quail, and American bison, often called buffalo. Blackfoot hunters used bows, arrows, spears, and guns to kill their prey.

    Buffalo were an important food source for the Blackfoot. Hunters who used spears or arrows had to get close to a buffalo to kill one. To do this, Blackfoot hunters covered themselves with a buffalo **hide**. They approached the herd from downwind so the animals could not smell their scent. This helped hunters get close enough to kill a buffalo.

    Sometimes the Blackfoot used buffalo jumps. Hunters herded the buffalo into a lane that ended with a steep cliff. When the buffalo stampeded down the lane, they ran off the cliff. Beneath the cliff, other hunters and women waited to harvest the animals.

Buffalo provided much of the Blackfoot's meat. People either ate the meat fresh or dried it for later use. They mixed the dried meat with wild berries, cherries, and buffalo fat to make pemmican (PEM-ih-kan). Pemmican could be stored and eaten later during travels.

The Blackfoot's only crop was tobacco. They smoked the tobacco in pipes, to send their prayers of thanks to the Creator.

A Blackfoot hunter covered in buffalo hide sneaks up on his prey.

Homes

The Blackfoot lived in tipis. The women's societies were responsible for making, putting up, and taking down the tipis. To begin, the women used four wooden poles to make a cone-shaped frame. Then they filled out the frame with more poles.

Next the women stretched a cover made from buffalo **hides** across the frame. A tipi cover consisted of about 15 hides sewn together. Wooden pegs fastened the cover closed. Pegs also held the cover in place at the bottom of the tipi.

In the winter, women lined the tipis with additional buffalo skins. The Blackfoot used fire pits to heat their tipis. They slept on beds made with buffalo fur robes.

In the summer, the people rolled up the bottoms of their tipi covers. This allowed breezes to blow through and cool the inside of the tipi.

The Blackfoot used **travois** (trav-WAHZ) to carry tipis or other supplies. They made travois from two tipi poles. The

Blackfoot used dogs to pull the **travois**. Later, they used horses, which were able to carry more supplies and travel farther than dogs.

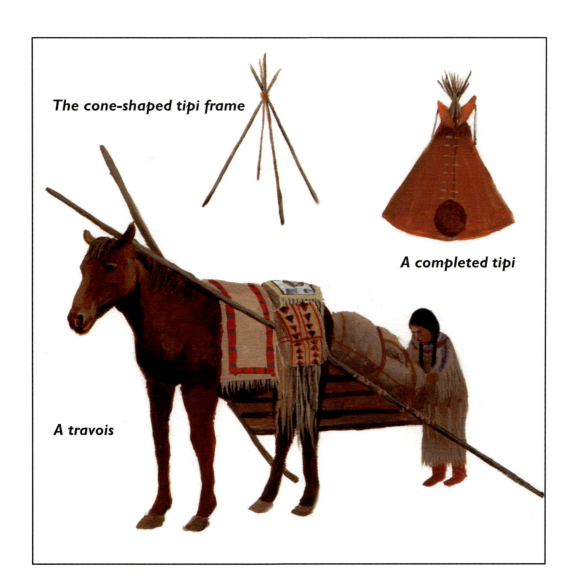

The cone-shaped tipi frame

A completed tipi

A travois

Clothing

Blackfoot men wore fringed buckskin shirts. The women sewed animal **hides** together to make the shirts. They decorated the shirts with **geometric** designs. They made the designs using porcupine **quills** or glass beads. Some shirts were also decorated with weasel tails, which were a sign of bravery.

Men also wore **breechcloths**. They wore thigh-high fringed **leggings**, too. The leggings protected their legs from brush and thorns while they were hunting.

Male elders and esteemed warriors sometimes wore special feather bonnets. They sewed eagle feathers onto each bonnet so it stood straight up and circled around the head. They hung white weasel pelts from the sides.

Blackfoot women wore long dresses made from elk hides. They decorated the dresses with fringes, quills, beads, elk teeth, or cowrie shells. They wore wide belts decorated with geometric designs around their waists. Women carried their **awls** and knives on their belts.

In the winter, both men and women wore buffalo-**hide** robes to keep warm. They wore black moccasins on their feet. Many people believe this is how the Blackfoot got their name.

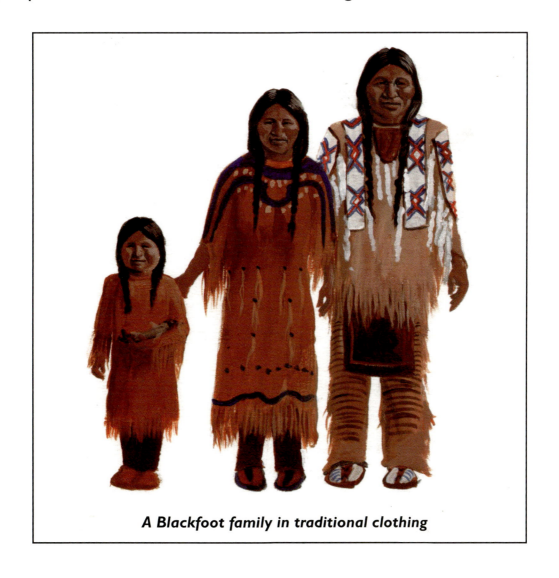

A Blackfoot family in traditional clothing

Crafts

The Blackfoot were excellent craftspeople. They used many natural materials in their crafts. They used rocks, plants, berries, clay, and ash to make paint. They also used the skins and other parts of animals such as the buffalo.

Men carved buffalo bones and horns into cups and other tools. They painted **pictographs** on the inside of buffalo robes, as a way to record important Blackfoot events. Sometimes the men spread a robe out on the ground. They told the people the stories painted on the robe.

Women painted pictographs and **geometric** designs on the inside of tipi liners and covers. They also decorated clothing, bags, and belts. They used bone needles and **sinew** thread to sew beads and porcupine **quills** into beautiful geometric designs.

A Blackfoot buffalo robe at the Plains Indians Museum

Family

In Blackfoot families, men could marry more than one woman. Sometimes a man married his first wife's sisters. They all lived together in one tipi.

The first wife had authority over the other wives. She was called his "sits beside him wife," because she always sat to her husband's left side. The other wives sat to the left of the first wife.

The women took care of the children. They made clothing, cooked, and preserved food for the winter. When the hunters killed an animal, the women butchered it using stone knives. Sometimes, women joined the warriors to protect the people.

Men hunted buffalo and other animals. They made the weapons needed for hunting and protection. They also made spoons, cups, and other tools from buffalo horns, bones, and **hides**. Men sometimes made their own clothing.

A Blackfoot man and his wives

Children

Blackfoot children were an important part of the family. The whole family taught and protected them. The children learned much by helping their parents.

Boys learned how to make bows and arrows. They also played a game with a spoked hoop wrapped in **rawhide**. The boys rolled the hoop along the ground. They shot arrows through the hoop as it rolled. This game sharpened the boys' hunting skills.

Girls learned how to cook, prepare buffalo **hides**, and do **quill** and bead work. They also learned how to sew together hides to make small tipis. The tipis were large enough for the girls to play inside. This taught them how to build, care for, and move tipis.

Both boys and girls each went through a **rite of passage.** The elders performed a ceremony and gave instructions on adulthood. The boys and girls also sought a vision. During the vision quest, a spirit guide sometimes came to the child. If it did, the child would have this guide to help him or her throughout life.

A Blackfoot boy meets his spirit guide.

Myths

The Blackfoot believe Napi (NAH-pee), or Old Man, created all living things. He gave humans and animals life. Napi also created land and food.

When the world first began, Napi created the mountains, hills, grasslands, and streams. He used clay to create birds and other animals. He created plants and trees.

Napi placed each animal, bird, and plant in a special place that it was suited for. The bighorn sheep have special hooves made to climb steep cliffs. So Napi placed them in the mountains. The pronghorn could run very fast. So Napi placed them on the open prairie.

Napi also made human shapes from clay. He blew breath onto them to give them life. He showed the humans how to live on the land, what to eat, and where to find plants to heal sickness.

Napi created the buffalo. He showed the Blackfoot how to kill buffalo and use them to make food, clothing, tipis, and tools.

When Napi had finished teaching the Blackfoot, he said he would always watch over the people. He walked westward. He turned to the people and said that some day he would return to the Blackfoot.

Napi

War

The Blackfoot were excellent warriors. During war, Blackfoot **bands** often joined together. The united warriors protected the people and land.

Warriors fought with many types of weapons. They used bows and arrows, stone knives, war clubs, and lances. The warriors made knife blades, arrowheads, and lance points from flint. They shaped them by hitting the flint with another rock.

Blackfoot men used shields for protection. They made the shields from stretched buffalo **rawhide**. The rawhide came from the thick skin on the back of a buffalo's neck. They painted the shields and their horses with protective drawings and symbols. The symbols came to the men in a dream or vision. They believed painting these special symbols on their shields and horses would protect them from harm.

A Blackfoot warrior could earn honors by counting coup on an enemy. When counting coup, a warrior touched a sleeping enemy or took his weapon. The Blackfoot believed it took greater courage to count coup on an enemy than to kill him. A man who counted coup could earn his way into a respected military society.

Blackfoot weapons

Contact with Europeans

Meriwether Lewis

Spanish explorers brought horses to North America in the 1500s. By the 1700s, the Blackfoot received horses through trade with other tribes. The Blackfoot called horses Elk Dogs. They had long legs like elk and carried loads like pack dogs. Horses allowed the Blackfoot to travel farther, and made hunting buffalo safer.

Europeans affected the Blackfoot way of life in other ways, too. They traded goods such as guns, blankets, and alcohol for **hides** and decorated clothing. They also brought diseases, such as smallpox. The Blackfoot did not have medicine or natural defenses against such diseases, and many people died.

In 1806, the Blackfoot met some men from the Lewis and Clark Expedition. A group of Blackfoot camped with Meriwether Lewis and his small party. Lewis told them their land was now a part of the United States. This upset the Blackfoot. So in the early morning, the Blackfoot tried to steal the group's weapons. Lewis shot two of the warriors.

In 1855, the Blackfoot and the United States government signed the Lamed Bull's Treaty. The treaty said the Blackfoot would receive food and trade goods if they allowed whites to travel across their lands. White settlers soon flooded into their lands.

In 1870, U.S. Major Eugene Baker led his troops to the Marias River. They were looking for a group of Blackfoot who had raided white settlers. They came across a peaceful **band** of Blackfoot and attacked them. Many innocent people were killed or captured. Today, this is remembered as the Baker or Marias **Massacre**.

White men hunted the buffalo to near extinction. By the winter of 1883-1884, the buffalo herds had disappeared. That winter, many Blackfoot starved to death.

A Blackfoot warrior speaks with Meriwether Lewis

Crowfoot

Issapo'mahkikaaw (isah-poh-mah-ki-kah) was a respected Blackfoot leader. He was born around 1830 in Alberta, Canada. He was courageous in battle. Once, he was wounded while fighting the Crow. This is how he earned the name Crowfoot.

Crowfoot was not born into a family of chiefs. But he proved to be a good leader. He was a good speaker, and was well respected. He eventually became a chief of the Siksika.

As chief, Crowfoot worked to ensure the health and safety of his people. He wanted the Blackfoot to stop drinking whiskey and other alcohol. He saw that his people were dying and being cheated.

In 1874, the North-West Mounted Police came to Blackfoot territory. Crowfoot knew they would stop the trade of alcohol. He spoke with his people. He convinced them that the Mounted Police would help the Blackfoot. The Mounted Police helped the Blackfoot reject alcohol and war with other tribes.

Crowfoot believed it was best for the Blackfoot to make peace with other tribes, as well as white settlers and traders. In 1877, he signed Treaty Seven with the Canadian government and other tribes. In 1885, he kept his people from participating in the North West Rebellion against the Canadian government. He died in 1890, after a long illness.

Crowfoot

The Blackfoot Today

Today, many Blackfoot live on **reservations**. The three Blackfoot reservations in Alberta, Canada, are the Siksika Reserve, the Blood Reserve, and the North Peigan Reserve. About 10,000 Blackfoot are enrolled with these reserves.

In the United States, the Blackfeet Reservation located in Montana is home to the Pikuni. This reservation has about 15,000 enrolled members.

The Blackfoot are working to protect their sacred lands. Areas such as the Badger Two Medicine area are disputed by the Blackfoot and those who wish to use it for development and drilling. The Blackfoot do not want such things to harm their sacred lands. They wish to preserve the environment for the future.

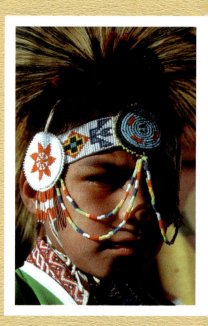

Blackfoot Native Americans wearing traditional headdresses

The Blackfoot are working to preserve their **culture**, too. Blackfoot elders teach young people the Blackfoot language and culture. The University of Lethbridge in Alberta, Canada, published a Blackfoot dictionary and grammar book.

A radio station was started to help preserve the Blackfoot language, stories, and traditional knowledge. The Head-Smashed In Buffalo Jump Interpretive Centre in Alberta, Canada, also provides information about the Blackfoot culture.

Chief Black Elk at Mount Rushmore

A Blackfoot Native American pushes a child in a wheelchair at the North American Indian Days celebration near Browning, Montana.

Even though the Blackfoot are divided by two countries, they are still family. Many Blackfoot come together for annual ceremonies and celebrations, such as the Sun Dance. This traditional, sacred summer event is private. The Blackfoot give prayers of thanks and perform other rituals.

Every July, the public is invited to social celebrations such as the North American Indian Days. During these social celebrations, people sing and dance to Blackfoot music.

A Blackfoot dancer wearing a feather headdress

The Blackfoot Nation of Montana sponsored the 34th annual North American Indian Nations Days. Tribes from the West and Midwest met for a Native American dance and drumming competition.

Glossary

awl - a pointed tool for marking or making small holes in materials such as leather or wood.

band - a number of persons acting together; a subgroup of a tribe.

breechcloth - a piece of hide or cloth, usually worn by men, that is wrapped between the legs and tied with a belt around the waist.

confederacy - a group of people joined together for a common purpose.

culture - the customs, arts, and tools of a nation or people at a certain time.

geometric - made up of straight lines, circles, and other simple shapes.

hide - an animal skin that is often thick and heavy.

leggings - coverings for the legs, usually made of cloth or leather.

massacre - the brutal killing of helpless or unresisting people or animals.

pictograph - a picture that represents a word or idea.

quill - a stiff, sharp hair or spine.

rawhide - untanned cattle hide.

reservation - a piece of land set aside by the government for Native Americans to live on.

rite of passage - an event or ceremony after which a child is considered an adult.

sinew - a band of tough fibers that joins a muscle to a bone.

travois - a frame of two wooden poles tied together over the back of an animal and allowed to drag on the ground. It was used to transport loads.

Web Sites

Head-Smashed In Buffalo Jump Interpretive Centre
http://www.head-smashed-in.com/

Blackfeet Nation
http://www.blackfeetnation.com

These sites are subject to change. Go to your favorite search engine and type in Blackfoot for more sites.

Index

A

art 14, 22

B

Badger Two Medicine 28
Baker, Major Eugene 25
Baker or Marias Massacre 25
bands 6, 22, 25
bead work 12, 14, 18
Blackfeet Reservation 28
Blood Reserve 28
buffalo 8, 9, 10, 13, 14, 16, 18, 20, 22, 24, 25

C

ceremonies 6, 7, 18, 30
chief 6, 7, 26
children 16, 18
clothing 12, 13, 16, 20
council of elders 6
counting coup 22, 23
crafts 14,
culture 29

D

diseases 24

E

Europeans 24
explorers 24

F

family 16, 18, 30
farming 9
food 6, 8, 9, 16, 18, 20, 25

G

games 18

H

Head-Smashed In Buffalo Jump Interpretive Centre 29
homelands 4, 5, 26, 28
hunting 8, 12, 16, 18, 24, 25

I

Issapo'mahkikaaw (Crowfoot) 26, 27

K

Kainai 4

L

Lamed Bull's Treaty 25
language 4, 29
Lewis and Clark Expedition 24
Lewis, Meriwether 24, 25

M

medicine 6, 20, 24
myths 20, 21

N

Napi 20, 21
Niitsitapii 4
North Peigan Reserve 28
North West Rebellion 27

P

pictographs 14
Pikuni 4, 28

Q

quill work 12, 14, 18

R

religion 6, 9, 30
reservations 28
rites of passage 18

S

Siksika 4, 26
Siksika Reserve 28
societies 6, 10, 23

T

tipi 10, 14, 16, 18, 20
trade 24, 25, 27
travel 9, 11, 24, 25
travois 10, 11
Treaty Seven 27

V

vision quest 18

W

war 22, 23, 25, 26
weapons 8, 16, 18, 22, 23, 24
white settlement 25, 27